GOOD BAD MOMS OF THE BIBLE

A Glimpse into Real Moms from the Bible for Busy Mamas Today

21-Day Devotional

by Shilah Goin

LITE Publishing
P.O. Box 581628
Elk Grove, CA 95758
www.litepublishing.com

Published in Elk Grove, California, by LITE Publishing
ISBN 978-0-9968298-4-7
Printed in the United States of America
First Edition

Table of Contents

INTRODUCTION

A little about me and what goodbadmoms is all about:

I got married at 19 years young after dating the guy for all of 5½ months. We had a miscarriage to start our marriage and moved seven times in three years. So to say the odds were stacked against us is an understatement. But God held us, helped us, and is still helping us everyday! Kiel and I are still madly in love 14 years, 3 more moves, 3 kids, and 3 dogs later.

We tried for 2½ years after the miscarriage to have a baby with no luck, which felt like a constant painful reminder of what we had lost. (I know this is a relatively short compared to some cases, but with infertility being so prevalent, I thought we were headed down a long dark road!)

Each month the negative test made me more bitter and sad. But thank God, He showed me a promise for children in the Bible and we soon got pregnant with our firstborn son, Ezekiel.

So naturally, I became the perfect mom!

Ha ha ha, NOT!

I remember as I held my baby the night we came home from the hospital saying to myself, "What were they thinking sending this baby home with me? I have no clue what I'm doing!"

I'm thankful I knew I could rely on God and His promises to continue to help me. He placed examples in the Bible to get me through each sleepless night, barf-covered outfit, temper tantrum, and knock down-drag out fight my precious angel babies would bring my way. These are some of the examples from various moms of the Bible that got me to the other side of each hard moment "momming" brings. We are not perfect moms! We all parent, learn, teach, and grow differently, and that's okay.

So let's look at an array of different moms who aren't perfect, just like us!

Day #1
MOTHER MARY KNOWS BEST

The wine supply ran out during the festivities, so Jesus' mother told him, "They have no more wine." "Dear woman, that's not our problem," Jesus replied. "My time has not yet come." But his mother told the servants, "Do whatever he tells you."

Standing nearby were six stone water jars, used for Jewish ceremonial washing. Each could hold twenty to thirty gallons. Jesus told the servants, "Fill the jars with water." When the jars had been filled, he said, "Now dip some out, and take it to the master of ceremonies." So the servants followed his instructions.

When the master of ceremonies tasted the water that was now wine, not knowing where it had come from (though, of course, the servants knew), he called the bridegroom over. "A host always serves the best wine first," he said. "Then, when everyone has had a lot to drink, he brings out the less expensive wine. But you have kept the best until now!"

This miraculous sign at Cana in Galilee was the first time Jesus revealed his glory. And his disciples believed in him.

– John 2:3-11 (NLT)

"You push your children too hard!"

"They are just kids; you expect too much out of them."

As a mom, have you heard these comments before? Well, I have!

Imagine this: Jesus says "My time has not come." Yet his mama says "Oh yes it has, buddy!" (Okay, maybe she did not say it exactly like that.)

But sometimes Mother really does know best! What would have happened if she went with her child's pace? What would have happened had she second-guessed herself? This was Jesus' first miracle! And his MAMA pushed him into it even when he thought he wasn't ready.

Don't get me wrong; I'm not saying let your 3-year-old walk across a busy street alone. But I am saying God even gave Jesus a mom; He created us to be moms! God knew children needed their mamas. God gave your children you! Please don't give up on what you think is right for your child based on others' opinions or even your child's wishes.

Day #2
HEAR ME ROAR-AR-AR-AR-ARRRRR

So Bathsheba went into the king's bedroom. (He was very old now, and Abishag was taking care of him.) Bathsheba bowed down before the king.

"What can I do for you?" he asked her. She replied, "My lord, you made a vow before the Lord your God when you said to me, 'Your son Solomon will surely be the next king and will sit on my throne.' And the king repeated his vow: "As surely as the Lord lives, who has rescued me from every danger, your son Solomon will be the next king and will sit on my throne this very day, just as I vowed to you before the Lord, the God of Israel."

– 1 Kings 1:15-17, 29-30 NLT

Bathsheba went to bat for her baby! She pleaded her son's case. If she had not gone to her husband, King David, one of his other sons would have become the next king. But "Mama Bear" happened and King Solomon went on to become one of the greatest, wisest, and by far the richest king Israel had ever had.

You are the one who will step up to the plate for your child. You know the gifts and talents your child has. God gave us the right as moms to support, campaign, and advocate for our children. I encourage you to be aware that, even though it's good for children to speak for themselves, at times it's okay to be their spokesperson. Mama Bear on!

Day #3
SECOND CHANCES

Late one afternoon, after his midday rest, David got out of bed and was walking on the roof of the palace. As he looked out over the city, he noticed a woman of unusual beauty taking a bath. He sent someone to find out who she was, and he was told, "She is Bathsheba, the daughter of Eliam and the wife of Uriah the Hittite." Then David sent messengers to get her; and when she came to the palace, he slept with her. She had just completed the purification rites after having her menstrual period. Then she returned home. Later, when Bathsheba discovered that she was pregnant, she sent David a message, saying, "I'm pregnant."

....So the next morning David wrote a letter to Joab and gave it to Uriah to deliver. The letter instructed Joab, "Station Uriah on the front lines where the battle is fiercest. Then pull back so that he will be killed." So Joab assigned Uriah to a spot close to the city wall where he knew the enemy's strongest men were fighting. And when the enemy soldiers came out of the city to fight, Uriah the Hittite was killed along with several other Israelite soldiers.

....When the period of mourning was over, David sent for her and brought her to the palace, and she became one of his wives. Then she gave birth to a son. But the Lord was displeased with what David had done.

....Then David confessed to Nathan, "I have sinned against the Lord." Nathan replied, "Yes, but the Lord has forgiven you, and you won't die for this sin.

....When David saw them whispering, he realized what had happened. "Is the child dead?" he asked. "Yes," they replied, "he is dead."

....Then David comforted his wife, Bathsheba, and went in to her and lay with her, and she bore a son, and he called his name Solomon. And the Lord loved him.

– 2 Samuel 11:2-5,14-17,27, 2 Samuel 12:13,19,24 (NLT)

REALLY long story short…King David had an affair with a married woman named Bathsheba, making her preggers. The king tried to hide it by having her hubby come home from war and tried to get him to sleep with her, twice. But when that plot failed, David had her husband murdered. An affair, unwed pregnancy, and murder? Not off to a good start here!

Next, she married King David, but in the end the two lost their son to illness. Talk about a telanovela! The beginning of her motherhood was not a pretty picture! I'm sure the circumstances could not have felt any worse.

But they repented! God forgave them just like God will forgive ANYTHING we have done when we turn to Him.

Thankfully, it did not end there for that mama. God gave her another son (Solomon) and he became a rich and wise King of Israel.

God gives second chances no matter the past circumstances. If you have a past, leave it there! Ask for forgiveness from God, Go forward knowing God loves you and your children, and wants the best for you! Today is a start to your new amazing motherhood. Happy second chancing, mamas!

Day #4
"CAUSE I'M HAPPY" ESSENTIAL OIL
(Clap along ♫)

He gives the childless woman a family, making her a happy mother, Praise the lord.

– Psalms 113:9 (NLT)

Two points I want to make today. First, if you don't have a child but want one...please, please, please know that God, over and over again, gave children to barren women. He will and can do it again for you. Pray and ask him for a child; believe and know He wants to do it for you. He loves you so much he wants to make you a happy mom.

Secondly, we are moms. Most times we are thankful and happy about it, while other moments, we want to scream into our pillows about the sock they never pick up even after telling them 378 times. And I believe that's okay, but we are also supposed to praise God for our families. When we praise God for our families, he will remind us why we are happy to have them (because we need to be reminded about that at times).

Also, when we praise God, he shows up, and he can change the atmosphere in our homes. It's like praising Him for our children is our happy essential oil defuser.

Example: Thank you God for my children. Thank you for their health. I thank you for their smiles. I ask that you show me their talents and passions. I ask that you help me in the rough times and change the atmosphere to a peaceful loving one. Help me parent them the way you want me to.

Day #5
MAMA TO MORE

But on the way, Naomi said to her two daughters-in-law, "Go back to your mothers' homes. And may the Lord reward you for your kindness to your husbands and to me."

"No," they said. "We want to go with you to your people."

"No, my daughters, return to your parents' homes, for I am too old to marry again. And even if it were possible, and I were to get married tonight and bear sons, then what?"

And again they wept together, and Orpah kissed her mother-in-law good-bye. But Ruth clung tightly to Naomi.

– Ruth 1:8,10,12,14 (NLT)

After losing her husband and her two sons, Naomi then had two widowed daughter-in-laws to take care of. She helped place one daughter-in-law back safely in her land, but one daughter-in-law would not leave and still clung to her. And so they began a new life together.

Sometimes in life there will be children along the way who may not be our own flesh and blood, but they still will need us to be a mother. (It may even be the kid who make us think, "who the heck is your mother, little brat?" Oops, too real? Sorry, back on topic.) God placed a lot of examples in the Bible about moms caring for children who weren't their natural-born children. Some of these kids in your life will have a mom already but may need extra momming…

starting with prayer, all the way to play time and in between. I encourage you to keep an eye out for someone God has placed in your life for whom you can make a difference in their life situation.

Day #6
LET IT GO!

But Naomi said, "Turn back, my daughters; why will you go with me? Have I yet sons in my womb that they may become your husbands? Turn back, my daughters; go your way, for I am too old to have a husband. If I should say I have hope, even if I should have a husband this night and should bear sons, would you therefore wait till they were grown? Would you therefore refrain from marrying?"

– Ruth 1:11-13 (ESV)

We see Naomi in this situation think of how she can help her daughter-in-laws. She feels pressure to take care of the situation. She comes up with plans that, once thought out, are a obvious no-go. **Reacting based mostly on pressure could lead to wrong decisions.**

Who doesn't relate? Come on now, be honest?

How many times have I come up with a plan just to ease the pressure? A LOT! My point here is that there will be times when we need to go with God's plan—not ours. Don't get me wrong; after Naomi gave up making all these plans for her daughters, the next thing they did was all sit down and cry together. And that's okay too! Letting go may not be easy and sometimes it may lead to tears...but stay strong in knowing that God's got you and your children and He has a good plan for you.

He did not call you to fix everything wrong with your children; he called you to love them and raise them to love God.

Find out what happens in the next chapter of these ladies' lives tomorrow.

Day #7
ADULT CHILD

Then she fell on her face, bowing to the ground, and said to him, "Why have I found favor in your eyes, that you should take notice of me, since I am a foreigner?" But Boaz answered her, "All that you have done for your mother-in-law (Naomi) since the death of your husband has been fully told to me, and how you left your father and mother and your native land and came to a people that you did not know before. The Lord repay you for what you have done, and a full reward be given you by the Lord, the God of Israel, under whose wings you have come to take refuge!" Then she said, "I have found favor in your eyes, my lord, for you have comforted me and spoken kindly to your servant, though I am not one of your servants."

– Ruth 2:10-13 (ESV)

This one is HARD for me. So I'm mostly talking to me here when I say this: sometimes being a good mom and training up a child in the way he/she should go is leading by example—by being a good adult child.

For Ruth, honoring her mother-in-law set a precedent and led to her marriage to a generous—and might I add, loaded ($$)—guy named Boaz. It also led to her having a son who would end up being King David's grandfather. She modeled how to be a good child. Ruth's actions of being a daughter who honored her mom-in-law made her famous and gained her favor with others around her. Through this example of how to be a good daughter, she managed to pass down a legacy of godly parenting and honor for parents.

What we do today, concerning not only our children but also our parents, has a lasting generational effect.

Day #8
A STRONG MAN'S STRONG MOM

"No razor shall come upon his head, for the child shall be a Nazirite to God from the womb, and he shall begin to save Israel from the hand of the Philistines."

"Now when your words come true, what is to be the child's manner of life, and what is his mission?" And the angel of the Lord said to Manoah, "Of all that I said to the woman let her be careful. She may not eat of anything that comes from the vine, neither let her drink wine or strong drink, or eat any unclean thing. All that I commanded her let her observe."

– Judges 13:5,12-14 (ESV)

Samson's mama must have been one strong woman! Can you imagine chasing little Samson around? If you don't know, he was one of the strongest men ever recorded. I mean, come on; he beat up like a ton of guys and ripped an attacking lion apart with only his hands. In these scriptures we note that the angel said to "be careful" to Samson's mom. The word "careful" could also mean "vigilant, meticulous, and diligent."* I imagine this mama worked hard to obey what God had for her to do.

In this passage we see that as moms we are commanded to be "careful" to "observe" what God has for us to do. First, let me say that if God asked us to do it, He gives us the grace and mercy to do it! Second, This "observe" or "obedience to God's plan" is what will produce good things in our life and our children's lives. If God wants us

to do it then it is good! And thank God, He will help to make us strong enough to do it!

*Google dictionary

Day #9
LET GO AND LET GOD

Now a man from the house of Levi went and took as his wife a Levite woman. The woman conceived and bore a son, and when she saw that he was a fine child, she hid him three months. When she could hide him no longer, she took for him a basket made of bulrushes and daubed it with bitumen and pitch. She put the child in it and placed it among the reeds by the river bank.

– Exodus 2:1-3 (ESV)

The woman in these scriptures was named Jochebed; she was Moses' mom. She gave birth and loved him instantly, but there was a law that dictated they kill all baby boys born during this time. So she did what she could do for as long as she could; she hid him. But when that was no longer an option, she got a plan from God and let Him take over the situation to keep him safe.

As moms, most of us do everything we can to ensure a good life for our kids, but as they get older, we find that sometimes we can't step in and make everything happy or perfect for them. There is heartbreak, disappointment, and loss that we can't always shield our children from. But there still is hope!

We see in this story that God took over when this mama could do no more. He'll do the same for us! When we've done what we can, we can "let go and let God."

*See what's next for Moses and how he comes out of the river tomorrow.

Day #10
WORRY 'BOUT YOURSELF

And his sister stood at a distance to know what would be done to him.

Then Pharaoh's daughter went down to the Nile to bathe, and her attendants were walking along the riverbank. She saw the basket among the reeds and sent her female slave to get it. She opened it and saw the baby. He was crying, and she felt sorry for him. "This is one of the Hebrew babies," she said. Then his sister said to Pharaoh's daughter, "Shall I go and call you a nurse from the Hebrew women to nurse the child for you?" And Pharaoh's daughter said to her, "Go." So the girl went and called the child's mother.

– Exodus 2:4-8 (ESV)

What if? I play this game often. So "what if" Moses' mom did not let her daughter, Miriam, follow and help Moses in this situation? I imagine Jochebed may have never seen Moses again and she would not have had the chance to help raise him and nurse him.

Because Jochebed let her daughter help her, Moses ended up being saved from certain death (alligators, snakes, drowning, oh my!—it all sounds terrible) and set up for a good life. Isn't that what all moms want for their kids? A good life?

It seems to me that children are sometimes more sensitive to God's leading than we are. Our children are blessed with special gifts and talents from God, and he uses them to accomplish His perfect and amazing will. If we let

them use these gifts, it will benefit not only them, but us as well. Looking for their talents and emphasizing them will build lasting effects in their lives. It brings a feeling of accomplishment when we know we are being used by God. Letting our children experience the joy of being used by God, even at a young age, will be life-changing. Our children's talents, passion, and gifts can bring joy and peace into our lives that we would miss out on otherwise.

Day #11
MOM PRESSURE

Then the man—Adam—named his wife Eve, because she would be the mother of all who live.

– Genesis 3:20 (NLT)

MOTHER TO ALL? Um, okay. No pressure here!

There is so much pressure today to be the best mom ever! To go all organic, no GMO, no peanuts, no gluten, no sugar, and the list goes on. The pressure Eve must have felt can't even be comprehended. Reading further, we see that she ended up with a murderer for a son. Yikes, what a screw-up mom! Right? Isn't this what we would all think of her in today's world? But the truth is she also raised a son named Abel and later a son named Seth who were known for loving and serving God with their whole hearts.

Let's let go of all the labels. Let go of the pressure to be Mother Teresa. Sometimes we can be a Pinterest mom and sometimes we are an Amazon Prime mom. And both are okay! Just be a mom! Be a mother that you're okay with, whether anyone else approves or not. Be a mother that your children will remember as loving.

Day #12
OWN YOUR PARENTING STYLE

Now Adam knew Eve his wife, and she conceived and bore Cain, saying, "I have gotten a man with the help of the Lord." And again, she bore his brother Abel. Now Abel was a keeper of sheep, and Cain a worker of the ground.

– Genesis 4:1-2 (KJV)

So this mama had two boys at this point. That's a workout in itself! One was a shepherd and one a farmer. What we notice is that Eve raised these boys to become what worked best for them as individuals.

I struggle sometimes imagining all three of my kids as what I want them to be, and not always what they actually should be. I always imagine something safe and well-paying! So basically a CEO of a big company, lots of money, and a private jet….

Actually, on second thought, maybe the jet's not safe enough!

I know deep down that God has something unique and special for each of my children. And it's okay to have them follow different paths. It's okay to even parent them differently based upon the individual needs of the child. I didn't say love them differently; I just mean let them take the path God has for them. God's path will always

be better and greater than any path we could choose for them.

Day #13
PEACE FOR MAMA

In her deep anguish Hannah prayed to the Lord, weeping bitterly. And she made a vow, saying, "Lord Almighty, if you will only look on your servant's misery and remember me, and not forget your servant but give her a son, then I will give him to the Lord for all the days of his life, and no razor will ever be used on his head."

Eli answered, "Go in peace, and may the God of Israel grant you what you have asked of him." She said, "May your servant find favor in your eyes." Then she went her way and ate something, and her face was no longer downcast. Early the next morning they arose and worshiped before the Lord and then went back to their home at Ramah. Elkanah made love to his wife Hannah, and the Lord remembered her. So in the course of time Hannah became pregnant and gave birth to a son. She named him Samuel, saying, "Because I asked the Lord for him."

– 1 Samuel 1:10-11,17-20 (NIV)

We start this story with a woman dealing with infertility. It's an extremely personal and devastating topic today. In this case, she's so distraught that she prays and weeps bitterly—not just in private, but even in front of Eli the priest. In the desperate moment of heartfelt prayer, she makes a vow to dedicate her son to God. Eli gives her the answer from God she's been looking for. But even though Hannah was not any more "pregnant" after hearing this answer than she was when she came in crying, she believed God heard her prayer. She was given peace and joy before she received a baby. Her prayer and God's answer changed her outlook even before she saw any evidence of change.

God answers our prayers today, too! Whatever we are facing in our #momlife, we can have faith that God hears our prayer and that prayer brings about the change needed for joy and peace.

Then comes the proof.

Prayer cycle:

Pray.
God answers.
Peace and joy come.
Then change and proof come.

Day #14
HUSBANDS SAY THE DARNEDEST THINGS

Then Abraham bowed down to the ground, but he laughed to himself in disbelief. "How could I become a father at the age of 100?" he thought. "And how can Sarah have a baby when she is ninety years old?"

But God replied, "No—Sarah, your wife, will give birth to a son for you. You will name him Isaac, and I will confirm my covenant with him and his descendants as an everlasting covenant."

– Genesis 17:17,19 (NLT)

So I know all of our lovely husbands are just so perfectly amazing and just never say anything stupid, right?

But every once in a while I look at mine, dumbfounded, and say, "Really, honey? Shut your face." Especially if he were to ever joke about me being old! He may even get socked in the arm! Or at least get some leg hair pulled out!

Okay, but in all seriousness, if you are called to be a mom, then you are equipped, you are graced, and you are able to be a godly mom. No matter what people say about you. No matter what you think about yourself. No matter what your oblivious husband says while putting his foot in his mouth. It does not matter if someone else doubts your ability to be a good mother. You, working together with God, are able to be the parent you need to be.

You and God's mercy and grace together enable you to be the right mom for your child's needs, no matter what!

Day #15
GOOD OLD DAYS

The angel said to him, "Zacharias, do not be afraid. Your prayer has been heard. Your wife Elizabeth will give birth to a son. You are to name him John...."

Some time later Elizabeth knew she was to become a mother. She kept herself hidden for five months. She said, "This is what the Lord has done for me. He has looked on me and has taken away my shame from among men."

– Luke 1:13,24-25 (NLV)

We all have those hair-pulling days! Those "I just need like 5 minutes of silence please!" days. Or those days when we just want to pee all by ourselves.

BUT, let's remember back to that day when we fell in love with our babies. Whether that was when we saw those two pink lines on a stick covered in pee (probably the last time we went to the bathroom alone), or whether it was when we looked at that beautiful newborn baby's face covered in white sticky stuff after the doctor handed him (or her) to us. No matter when the moment occurred, there was love and gratefulness. I know it's hard in the stressful chaos, but maybe when we are walking through a rough day, we should try to picture a moment in our lives and be grateful for it.

Opening our mouths in thanksgiving to God will help change our attitude. And let's face it—sometimes half of the

reasons we have stressful days are because of our attitude and how we look at things.

In Luke 1, Elizabeth could have been mad about having to hide herself away. (No girls' nights out with our mom bestie? What?) But instead she chose a grateful tone.

Thankfulness can help change our perspective in a bad moment.

Day #16
AWKWARD SITCH

When the Lord saw that Leah was unloved, he enabled her to have children, but Rachel could not conceive. So Leah became pregnant and gave birth to a son. She named him Reuben, for she said, "The Lord has noticed my misery, and now my husband will love me."

She soon became pregnant again and gave birth to another son. She named him Simeon, for she said, "The Lord heard that I was unloved and has given me another son."

Then she became pregnant a third time and gave birth to another son. He was named Levi, for she said, "Surely this time my husband will feel affection for me, since I have given him three sons!"

Once again Leah became pregnant and gave birth to another son. She named him Judah, for she said, "Now I will praise the Lord!" And then she stopped having children.

– Genesis 29:31-35 (NLT)

Okay, mamas, what I am about to say here is a hard topic, but let's dive in. We see in these scriptures a story of a woman in a loveless marriage. We next see her over and over and over and over again try to use her children to gain and control her husband's affections.

Yikes! The heartache she must be going through! The betrayal she felt from her father and husband for this forced marriage was intense, I'm sure. The loneliness, I can't even imagine. I am not trying to belittle rough situations by any means! But what I want to point out here is that this scheme of putting the children in the middle of a bad situation never worked

for her. Trying to use the kids to manipulate her husband did not bring the results she desired.

As mothers, I encourage all of us to make sure we are not using our children in a way that is not healthy for them. Thankfully we have a Heavenly Father whom we can cry out to. God can help you win your husband's heart back better than any scheme. Crying out to God in any situation will always work better than putting a child in an unhealthy or compromising place.

Day #17
👍 THUMBS UP 👍

When Rachel saw that she wasn't having any children for Jacob, she became jealous of her sister….Then Rachel told him, "Take my maid, Bilhah, and sleep with her. She will bear children for me, and through her I can have a family, too." Bilhah became pregnant and presented him with a son. Rachel named him Dan, for she said, "God has vindicated me! He has heard my request and given me a son." Meanwhile, Leah realized that she wasn't getting pregnant anymore, so she took her servant, Zilpah, and gave her to Jacob as a wife.

Soon Zilpah presented him with a son. Leah named him Gad, for she said, "How fortunate I am!" Then Zilpah gave Jacob a second son. And Leah named him Asher, for she said, "What joy is mine! Now the other women will celebrate with me."

– Genesis 30:1,3,5-6,9-13 (NLT)

Earlier in the story we read that Leah had already had four of her own children. Rachel and Leah both tried to outdo each other in this story. But here's the kicker: Verse 13 says "now the other women will celebrate with me."

For Leah it was not about her children or even her personal joy, but it was about more accolades from her peers. Sometimes, that can sum up a lot of our choices today as moms!

How much do we do in today's society just to get other moms to notice? What do we do to get more likes on Instagram and Facebook? How often do we make decisions based on the latest trend or staying on the top of the PTA popularity

contest? Let's start living for what brings us peace and joy and stop living for what brings us more Facebook thumbs up.

Day #18
MOM JELLY

When Rachel saw that she wasn't having any children for Jacob, she became jealous of her sister. She pleaded with Jacob, "Give me children, or I'll die!"

Then Rachel told him, "Take my maid, Bilhah, and sleep with her. She will bear children for me, and through her I can have a family, too." So Rachel gave her servant, Bilhah, to Jacob as a wife, and he slept with her.

Bilhah became pregnant and presented him with a son. Rachel named him Dan,for she said, "God has vindicated me! He has heard my request and given me a son."

Then Bilhah became pregnant again and gave Jacob a second son. Rachel named him Naphtali, for she said, "I have struggled hard withmy sister, and I'm winning!"

– Genesis 30:1,3-8 (NLT)

Did I read that right? Verse 8, "I have struggled hard with my sister, and I'm winning!" Mom jealousy…ever heard of that one? That's what Rachel and Leah had going on here.

We talked about Leah wanting more "mom likes." Now we see that Rachel just wanted to win the baby race! Rachel got jealous and finagled a way to keep up appearances and win the "who's better" battle that we moms can sometimes struggle with. Whether you have one child or 15 children (God help you), please, please know you are enough! We don't have to look at someone else's supposed greener grass and desire it. We can choose to say, "what we have is great for

us." I'm not saying we can't ask God for more, but let's try to focus on winning for our children, not just winning the race against someone else. You are enough!

Day #19
REACT OR RESPOND

When Jesus was twelve years old, they attended the festival as usual. After the celebration was over, they started home to Nazareth, but Jesus stayed behind in Jerusalem. His parents didn't miss him at first...

When they couldn't find him, they went back to Jerusalem to search for him there. Three days later they finally discovered him in the Temple, sitting among the religious teachers, listening to them and asking questions. All who heard him were amazed at his understanding and his answers. His parents didn't know what to think. "Son," his mother said to him, "why have you done this to us? Your father and I have been frantic, searching for you everywhere." "But why did you need to search?" he asked. "Didn't you know that I must be in my Father's house?" But they didn't understand what he meant.

Then he returned to Nazareth with them and was obedient to them. And his mother stored all these things in her heart. Jesus grew in wisdom and stature, and in favor with God and with people.

– Luke 2:42-43, 45-52 (NLT)

Putting myself in Mary's shoes, I think my kid would never, ever, ever be allowed to leave my side again. I'd probably buy those backpack leashes and make my kid wear it until he was 32 years old.

But this passage says that Mary stored all these things in her heart.

We see her respond to this scary-as-all-get-out situation. She could have reacted terribly (like I do most of the time—but hey, I'm working on it). She could have ripped him a new one, spanked his little booty till it hurt to walk, grounded him for a year, or took away his PlayStation for a week (oh wait, wrong century)…. She could have reacted, but instead she responded. She let God stir her heart and she took on God's thoughts about the situation. And we see it worked out for her. Jesus grew in wisdom and stature and favor!

I endeavor to start responding the way God wants me to, not just reacting the way my emotions want me to.

Prayer: Heavenly Father, I ask that you help me respond to stressful situations with your wisdom and perspective. Stir your thoughts on the inside of me. Help me control my emotions and guide my children with godly love.

Day #20
MOM'S BACKUP PLAN

Children obey your parents in the Lord, for this is right.

– Ephesians 6:1 (NIV)

We all need a little support and backup sometimes. In movies, when you've unloaded your gun and the creepy green swamp monster is still attacking, you pull out your backup gun (which just so happens to be bigger than the first one) and pull the trigger. "Say hello to my little friend." The backup won the day!

Sometimes I feel alone in this mom life. Sometimes I feel like I just want someone or something to back me up when I'm feeling discouraged. Well, this scripture is the backup for me. When all else has failed to get my children to listen, obey, or respect, I turn to this verse and read it out loud to them. When I let them know that it is not just me asking them to obey, it has a weight to it that their little spirits understand. They understand that God is also asking them to obey. It makes a huge difference in their response and I suddenly don't feel alone in trying to raise wise, happy, and successful children.

Day #21
LISTEN AND OBEY

If you are willing and obedient, you will have the best of the land.

– Isaiah 1:19 (AMP)

So this is a two-way street. Of course I use this scripture to let my children know that when they have a good attitude, listen, and obey, they get rewarded. And then sometimes I'll even take them to Taco Bell as a reward, and I don't have to make dinner, so it's a win-win (hey, it's called good BAD moms for a reason).

But also this is for us moms. When we have an open heart to listen to and obey the Bible on how we should do this momming thing, it opens us up to the best parenting that we have to offer. While we are obeying, we can be certain we will get "the best of the land" (in other words, a blessing). Believe me, I want the best house, car, job, etc., but I for sure want the best children too. This calling to be willing and obedient has a great blessing that tags along with it. I want the best for me and for my children, so I will endeavor to be willing and obedient with respect to how God wants me to parent.

I hope you have enjoyed the Good Bad Moms of the Bible 21-Day study! I pray it helps you keep #momming the way God has graced you to mom! Here's a bonus just for you, mama, because you rock this #momlife!

Bonus Day:
CONTROVERSIAL PARENTING TAG

The rod and reproof (godly instruction) give wisdom, but a child who gets his own way brings shame to his mother.

– Proverbs 29:15 (AMP)

Hot topic, I know! But here goes. Reproof means to have checked and then check again to re-proof. Like proofread but re-proofread. Proverbs 29 shows us that the reproof is godly instruction. I'd have to say that out of all the things I could wish for my children, wisdom would be at the top of the list (right after their ability to actually clean their rooms, but hey, I can't be too choosy, right?).

So if I don't want to be embarrassed by them when they get older, I am going to raise them with godly instruction. I am going to tell them exactly what the Bible says about them. I am going to use the Bible as my backup. I am going to raise them using the word of God as a guideline and even show them in the Word where it tells me to! I am going to reprove them knowing that it gives them wisdom!

I have a promise from God in Proverbs 22:6 that says "Train up a child in the way he should go, and when he is old, he will not depart from it."

THANK YOU, MAMAS

Thank you for taking the time these last 21 days to grow in grace for this #momlife. I know God has given you everything you need to parent your children to grow into blessings and become full of wisdom. I pray that this has helped you in some way. I also pray that at some point this week you can go to the bathroom by yourself at least once and can sneak a cookie without having to share it! (Maybe not at the same time though.) I believe that as you go into this next chapter of parenting, you will see that God has amazing things in store for you!

I can't even tell you how much fun I had writing this and how much I need this every. single. day. in my momming life. God is still working on and in me to be the mom my children need and deserve. Thank you for letting Good Bad Moms of the Bible be a part of the blessing God has coming your way.

KEEP MOMMING THE BIBLE WAY!

Shilah Goin

ABOUT THE AUTHOR

Shilah Goin is a stay-at-home mom of three children from ages 11, 8, and 6, respectively. When asked if she is going to have more children, she refrains from rigorously rolling her eyes and simply says "No, we were done at two kids; the third was just a surprise bonus." Okay, but in all seriousness, Shilah loves being a wife and mother. She also loves writing, fashion, singing, and getting away from it all somewhere in the woods!

Goodbadmoms was started by Shilah and her friend in January 2017. God has a special place in His heart for moms; it is Shilah's main goal to let other moms know that fact through Goodbadmoms. Goodbadmoms aims to show that with God's help, momming can be fun and enjoyable. With a flair for humor, Shilah tries to bring biblical truth in a clear and relevant way to reach busy moms.

www.ingramcontent.com/pod-product-compliance
Lightning Source LLC
Chambersburg PA
CBHW061058050726
47592CB00004B/1738

* 9 7 8 0 9 9 6 8 2 9 8 4 7 *